recorded by ....

THE EARTH IS THE VERY QUINTESSENCE OF THE HUMAN CONDITION.

—Hannah Arendt

GETTING STARTED

Whether you escape into the great outdoors for a quiet moment alone, or you set off on a family adventure, no walk in the woods is complete without the Naturalist's Journal. It's full of useful information, including National Park resources, a stargazing map, and a packing checklist for nature walk essentials, and it also provides plenty of room for your own treasured memories. The guided pages offer space to record the many details of your wilderness experiences, while blank pages inspire the painter, poet, scientist, or explorer in you. From a city park to a country meadow to your own backyard, take a break, grab your journal, and connect with the wonder of the natural world.

Like water,

we are truest

to our nature in repose.

—CYRIL CONNOLLY,
The Unquiet Grave

TOOLS FOR NATURE WALKING

- day pack
- first-aid kit
- magnifying glass
- field guides
- extra clothing
- water
- flashlight
  (check batteries and bulb)
- whistle
- matches

- hat
- granola bars
- money, including change
- pocket knife
- map
- wax paper or plastic baggies (for collecting and pressing leaves)
- compass and watch
- comfortable shoes
- bug repellent
- sunscreen
- sunglasses
- camera
- binoculars
- naturalist journal

TIPS FOR EACH SEASON

WINTER

- Winter is a great time to learn to identify, or "key out," trees and shrubs by their bark, buds, general shape, and branching habits. Find a tree identification guide that explains how.
- Find out what animals spend the winter in your area and what they might be up to. Mating? Raising young? Foraging? Hibernating?
- Are there any plants in bloom in your area in the winter? How are these winter-blooming plants pollinated?
- Bird nests that in other seasons are hidden by vegetation may now be visible.
- Look for animal tracks in snow and in muddy areas.
- Winter is also a great time to pay more attention to the light, the weather, and the stars.

SPRING

- Many plants have inconspicuous flowers that bloom before the leaves appear, so their pollen can be blown by the wind. Plants with showier flowers are generally trying to attract birds or insects. Notice when the various plants bloom in your area.
- Which birds arrive early in the season, and which arrive later? Are some birds just passing through on their way to other areas?
- Note the sounds of frogs and insects, especially at night.
- Spring is a great time to begin learning about edible wild plants.

- Take a nature walk on the beach. Collect an array of shells and sea glass to remember your trip.
- Take a walk in the same area at different times of day. Notice how the feeling of a place changes as the light and temperature change. You may also notice differences in the level of activity in the birds and other animals.
- At the shore you may notice more shorebirds foraging, fish jumping, or crabs scurrying, depending on the time of day.
- Summer is a great time to learn about edible wild plants.

- This is when foliage is best. Take a hike through a mountain trail.
- Which trees turn color first?
- Fall is the time to notice migrating birds and butterflies—they'll either be departing, arriving, or just passing through. If you pay attention, you'll begin to know when to expect them each year.
- Pick up some apple cider, a pumpkin pie, or some fresh fall vegetables from a farmstand on your way home.

Ovate

Oblanceolate

Elliptic

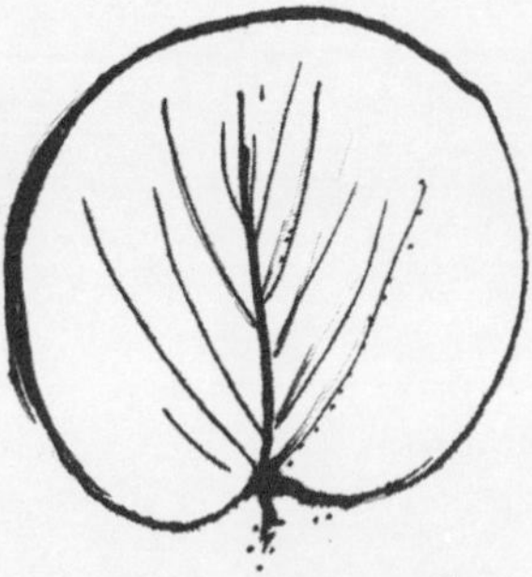

Rounded

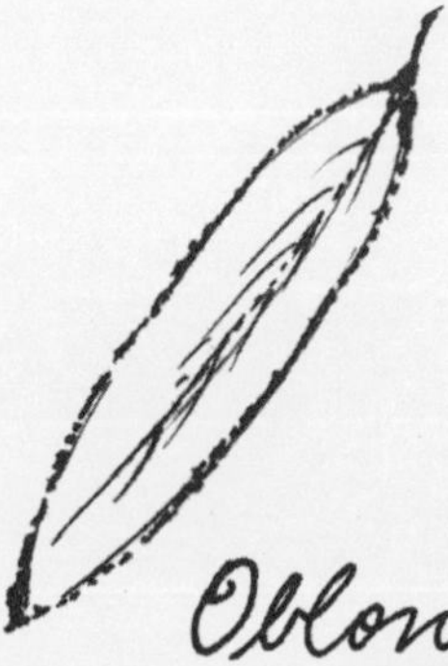

Oblong

LEAF SHAPES

Clove Hitch

Running Bowline

KNOT FORMATIONS

Square Knot

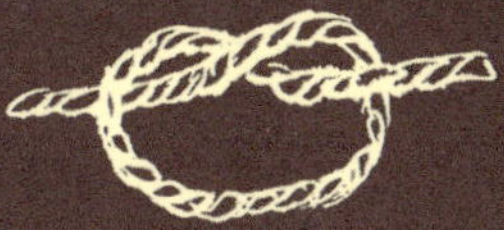

Overhand Knot

Granny Knot

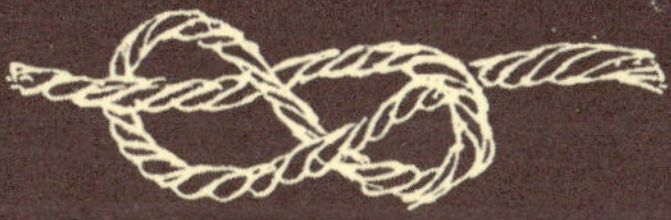

Figure-eight

Cow Hitch

Stratus

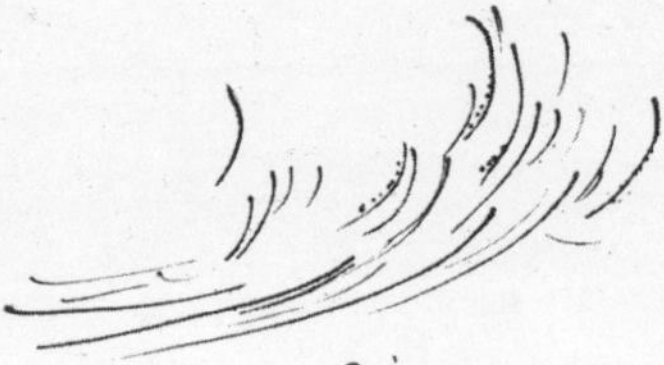

Cirrus

Cumulus

CLOUD FORMATIONS

Cirrostratus

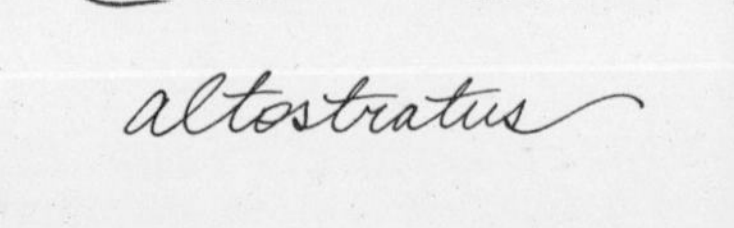

altostratus

altocumulus

cumulonimbus

Cirrocumulus

Stratocumulus

nimbostratus

Conch

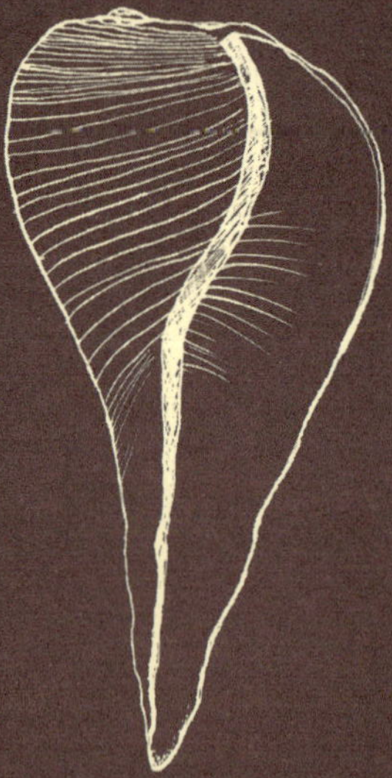

Paper Fig

Clam

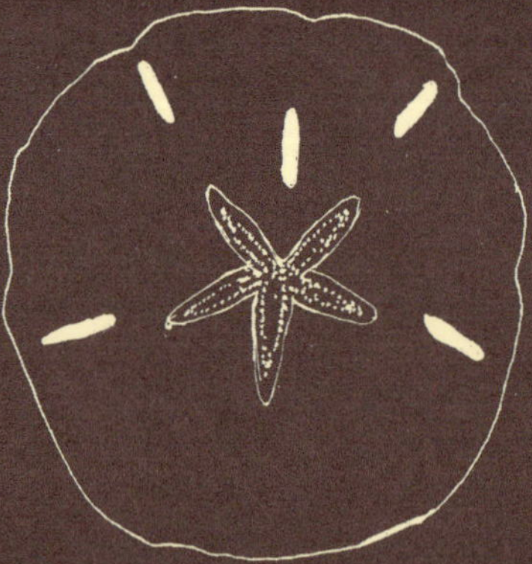

Sand Dollar

Snail

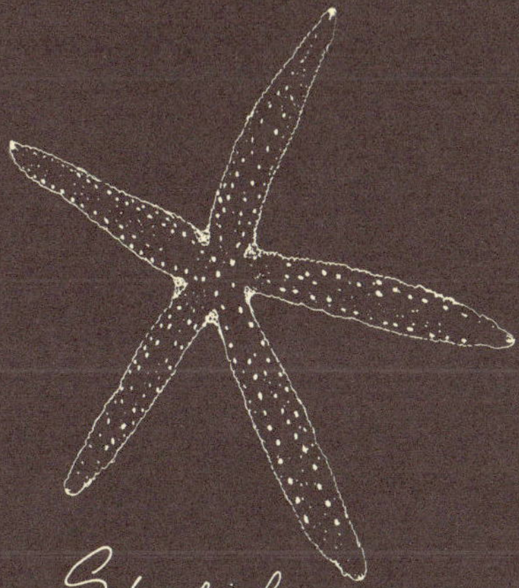

Starfish

BEACH FINDS

Mussel

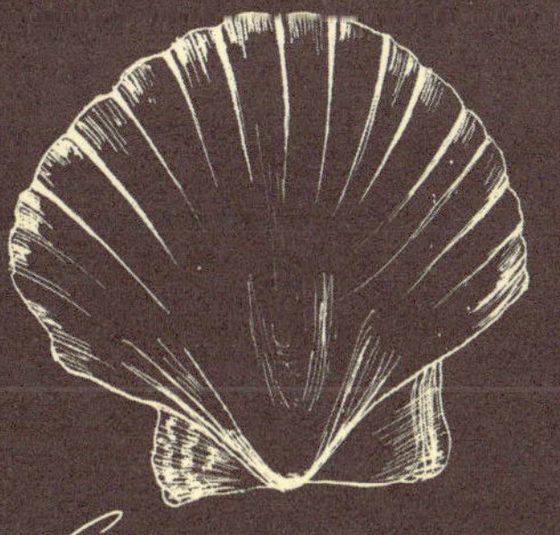

Scallop

where . . . .

. . . .

when . . . .

with whom . . . .

length of route . . . .

type of terrain . . . .

weather . . . .

cloud cover . . . .

major overhead plants . . . .

major underfoot plants . . . .

sunrise/sunset . . . .

latitude/longitude . . . .

elevation . . . .

point of departure . . . .

tide . . . .

birds seen or heard . . . .

. . . .

sounds . . . .

. . . .

sights . . . .

. . . .

synopsis . . . .

. . . .

. . . .

the first thing that strikes you . . . .

. . . .

. . . .

. . . .

. . . .

. . . .

If we do not find anything very pleasant,

at least we shall find something new.

—VOLTAIRE

track your trail

(you may also tape a trail map to this page)

things we saw and did

something surprising that happened • things to look fo

where . . . .

. . . .

when . . . .

with whom . . . .

length of route . . . .

type of terrain . . . .

weather . . . .

cloud cover . . . .

major overhead plants . . . .

major underfoot plants . . . .

sunrise/sunset . . . .

latitude/longitude . . . .

elevation . . . .

point of departure . . . .

tide . . . .

birds seen or heard . . . .

. . . .

sounds . . . .

. . . .

sights . . . .

. . . .

synopsis . . . .

. . . .

. . . .

the first thing that strikes you . . . .

. . . .

. . . .

. . . .

. . . .

. . . .

The sun was like a great visiting presence that stimulated and took its due from all animal energy. When it flung wide its cloak and stepped down over the edge of the fields at evening, it left behind it a spent and exhausted world.

—WILLA CATHER

track your trail

(you may also tape a trail map to this page)

things we saw

something surprising that happened • things to look f

where . . . .

. . . .

when . . . .

with whom . . . .

length of route . . . .

type of terrain . . . .

weather . . . .

cloud cover . . . .

major overhead plants . . . .

major underfoot plants . . . .

sunrise/sunset . . . .

latitude/longitude . . . .

elevation . . . .

point of departure . . . .

tide . . . .

birds seen or heard . . . .

. . . .

sounds . . . .

. . . .

sights . . . .

. . . .

synopsis . . . .

. . . .

. . . .

the first thing that strikes you . . . .

. . . .

. . . .

. . . .

. . . .

. . . .

Live in each season as it passes;
breathe the air, drink the drink,
taste the fruit, and resign
yourself to the influences of each.
Let them be your only diet drink and
botanical medicines.

—HENRY DAVID THOREAU

track your trail

(you may also tape a trail map to this page)

things we saw

something surprising that happened • things to look fo

nd remember • places to stop on the way . . . .

WALKING GUIDE

where . . . .

. . . .

when . . . .

with whom . . . .

length of route . . . .

type of terrain . . . .

weather . . . .

cloud cover . . . .

major overhead plants . . . .

major underfoot plants . . . .

sunrise/sunset . . . .

latitude/longitude . . . .

elevation . . . .

point of departure . . . .

tide . . . .

birds seen or heard . . . .

. . . .

sounds . . . .

. . . .

sights . . . .

. . . .

synopsis . . . .

. . . .

. . . .

the first thing that strikes you . . . .

. . . .

. . . .

. . . .

. . . .

. . . .

To sit in the shade on a fine day, and look upon verdure is the most perfect refreshment.

—JANE AUSTEN

track your trail

(you may also tape a trail map to this page)

things we saw

something surprising that happened • things to look fo

where . . . .

. . . .

when . . . .

with whom . . . .

length of route . . . .

type of terrain . . . .

weather . . . .

cloud cover . . . .

major overhead plants . . . .

major underfoot plants . . . .

sunrise/sunset . . . .

latitude/longitude . . . .

elevation . . . .

point of departure . . . .

tide . . . .

birds seen or heard . . . .

. . . .

sounds . . . .

. . . .

sights . . . .

. . . .

synopsis . . . .

. . . .

. . . .

the first thing that strikes you . . . .

. . . .

. . . .

. . . .

. . . .

. . . .

Each blade of grass has its spot on earth
whence it draws its life, its strength;
and so is man rooted to the land from which he
draws his faith together with his life.

—JOSEPH CONRAD, FROM *LORD JIM*

track your trail

(you may also tape a trail map to this page)

things we saw

something surprising that happened • things to look fo

WALKING GUIDE

where . . . .

. . . .

when . . . .

with whom . . . .

length of route . . . .

type of terrain . . . .

weather . . . .

cloud cover . . . .

major overhead plants . . . .

major underfoot plants . . . .

sunrise/sunset . . . .

latitude/longitude . . . .

elevation . . . .

point of departure . . . .

tide . . . .

birds seen or heard . . . .

. . . .

sounds . . . .

. . . .

sights . . . .

. . . .

synopsis . . . .

. . . .

. . . .

the first thing that strikes you . . . .

. . . .

. . . .

. . . .

. . . .

. . . .

Every flower is a soul blossoming in Nature.

—GÉRARD DE NERVAL

track your trail

(you may also tape a trail map to this page)

things we saw

something surprising that happened • things to look fo

d remember • places to stop on the way . . . .

where . . . .

. . . .

when . . . .

with whom . . . .

length of route . . . .

type of terrain . . . .

weather . . . .

cloud cover . . . .

major overhead plants . . . .

major underfoot plants . . . .

sunrise/sunset . . . .

latitude/longitude . . . .

elevation . . . .

point of departure . . . .

tide . . . .

birds seen or heard . . . .

. . . .

sounds . . . .

. . . .

sights . . . .

. . . .

synopsis . . . .

. . . .

. . . .

the first thing that strikes you . . . .

. . . .

. . . .

. . . .

. . . .

. . . .

One sees great things from the valley;

only small things from the peak.

—G.K. CHESTERTON

track your trail

(you may also tape a trail map to this page)

things we saw

something surprising that happened • things to look f

where . . . .

. . . .

when . . . .

with whom . . . .

length of route . . . .

type of terrain . . . .

weather . . . .

cloud cover . . . .

major overhead plants . . . .

major underfoot plants . . . .

sunrise/sunset . . . .

latitude/longitude . . . .

elevation . . . .

point of departure . . . .

tide . . . .

birds seen or heard . . . .

. . . .

sounds . . . .

. . . .

sights . . . .

. . . .

synopsis . . . .

. . . .

. . . .

the first thing that strikes you . . . .

. . . .

. . . .

. . . .

. . . .

. . . .

In this broad earth of ours,
Amid the measureless grossness and the slag,
Enclosed and safe within its central heart,
Nestles the seed perfection.

—WALT WHITMAN,
SONG OF THE UNIVERSAL

track your trail

(you may also tape a trail map to this page)

things we saw

something surprising that happened • things to look f

where . . . .

. . . .

when . . . .

with whom . . . .

length of route . . . .

type of terrain . . . .

weather . . . .

cloud cover . . . .

major overhead plants . . . .

major underfoot plants . . . .

sunrise/sunset . . . .

latitude/longitude . . . .

elevation . . . .

point of departure . . . .

tide . . . .

birds seen or heard . . . .

. . . .

sounds . . . .

. . . .

sights . . . .

. . . .

synopsis . . . .

. . . .

. . . .

the first thing that strikes you . . . .

. . . .

. . . .

. . . .

. . . .

. . . .

Nature, like man, sometimes weeps from gladness.

—BENJAMIN DISRAELI

track your trail

(you may also tape a trail map to this page)

things we saw

something surprising that happened • things to look f

where . . . .

. . . .

when . . . .

with whom . . . .

length of route . . . .

type of terrain . . . .

weather . . . .

cloud cover . . . .

major overhead plants . . . .

major underfoot plants . . . .

sunrise/sunset . . . .

latitude/longitude . . . .

elevation . . . .

point of departure . . . .

tide . . . .

birds seen or heard . . . .

. . . .

sounds . . . .

. . . .

sights . . . .

. . . .

synopsis . . . .

. . . .

. . . .

the first thing that strikes you . . . .

. . . .

. . . .

. . . .

. . . .

. . . .

The Brain—is wider than the Sky—.

—EMILY DICKINSON

track your trail

(you may also tape a trail map to this page)

things we saw

something surprising that happened • things to look f

where . . . .

. . . .

when . . . .

with whom . . . .

length of route . . . .

type of terrain . . . .

weather . . . .

cloud cover . . . .

major overhead plants . . . .

major underfoot plants . . . .

sunrise/sunset . . . .

latitude/longitude . . . .

elevation . . . .

point of departure . . . .

tide . . . .

birds seen or heard . . . .

. . . .

sounds . . . .

. . . .

sights . . . .

. . . .

synopsis . . . .

. . . .

. . . .

the first thing that strikes you . . . .

. . . .

. . . .

. . . .

. . . .

. . . .

Curiosity is one of the most permanent and certain characteristics of a vigorous intellect.

—SAMUEL JOHNSON

track your trail

(you may also tape a trail map to this page)

things we saw

something surprising that happened • things to look f

where . . . .

. . . .

when . . . .

with whom . . . .

length of route . . . .

type of terrain . . . .

weather . . . .

cloud cover . . . .

major overhead plants . . . .

major underfoot plants . . . .

sunrise/sunset . . . .

latitude/longitude . . . .

elevation . . . .

point of departure . . . .

tide . . . .

birds seen or heard . . . .

. . . .

sounds . . . .

. . . .

sights . . . .

. . . .

synopsis . . . .

. . . .

. . . .

the first thing that strikes you . . . .

. . . .

. . . .

. . . .

. . . .

. . . .

Beauty of whatever kind, in its supreme development, invariably excites the sensitive soul to tears.

—EDGAR ALLAN POE, "THE RATIONALE OF VERSE," IN *THE PIONEER*

track your trail

(you may also tape a trail map to this page)

things we saw

something surprising that happened • things to look

WALKING GUIDE

where . . . .

. . . .

when . . . .

with whom . . . .

length of route . . . .

type of terrain . . . .

weather . . . .

cloud cover . . . .

major overhead plants . . . .

major underfoot plants . . . .

sunrise/sunset . . . .

latitude/longitude . . . .

elevation . . . .

point of departure . . . .

tide . . . .

birds seen or heard . . . .

. . . .

sounds . . . .

. . . .

sights . . . .

. . . .

synopsis . . . .

. . . .

. . . .

the first thing that strikes you . . . .

. . . .

. . . .

. . . .

. . . .

. . . .

I like trees because they seem more resigned to the way they have to live than other things do.

—WILLA CATHER, *O PIONEERS!*

track your trail

(you may also tape a trail map to this page)

things we saw

something surprising that happened • things to look f

where . . . .

. . . .

when . . . .

with whom . . . .

length of route . . . .

type of terrain . . . .

weather . . . .

cloud cover . . . .

major overhead plants . . . .

major underfoot plants . . . .

sunrise/sunset . . . .

latitude/longitude . . . .

elevation . . . .

point of departure . . . .

tide . . . .

birds seen or heard . . . .

. . . .

sounds . . . .

. . . .

sights . . . .

. . . .

synopsis . . . .

. . . .

. . . .

the first thing that strikes you . . . .

. . . .

. . . .

. . . .

. . . .

. . . .

The light which puts out our eyes is darkness to us.

Only that day dawns to which we are awake.

There is more day to dawn.

The sun is but a morning star.

—HENRY DAVID THOREAU

track your trail

(you may also tape a trail map to this page)

things we saw

something surprising that happened • things to look

where . . . .

. . . .

when . . . .

with whom . . . .

length of route . . . .

type of terrain . . . .

weather . . . .

cloud cover . . . .

major overhead plants . . . .

major underfoot plants . . . .

sunrise/sunset . . . .

latitude/longitude . . . .

elevation . . . .

point of departure . . . .

tide . . . .

birds seen or heard . . . .

. . . .

sounds . . . .

. . . .

sights . . . .

. . . .

synopsis . . . .

. . . .

. . . .

the first thing that strikes you . . . .

. . . .

. . . .

. . . .

. . . .

. . . .

The sea possesses a power over one's moods that has the effect of a will. The sea can hypnotize. Nature in general can do so.

—HENRIK IBSEN

track your trail

(you may also tape a trail map to this page)

things we saw

something surprising that happened • things to look f

where . . . .

. . . .

when . . . .

with whom . . . .

length of route . . . .

type of terrain . . . .

weather . . . .

cloud cover . . . .

major overhead plants . . . .

major underfoot plants . . . .

sunrise/sunset . . . .

latitude/longitude . . . .

elevation . . . .

point of departure . . . .

tide . . . .

birds seen or heard . . . .

. . . .

sounds . . . .

. . . .

sights . . . .

. . . .

synopsis . . . .

. . . .

. . . .

the first thing that strikes you . . . .

. . . .

. . . .

. . . .

. . . .

. . . .

My favorite thing to do is to go

where I've never been.

—DIANE ARBUS

track your trail

(you may also tape a trail map to this page)

things we saw

something surprising that happened • things to look f

d remember • places to stop on the way . . . .

A man travels the world in search of what he needs and returns home to find it.

—GEORGE MOORE

NATIONAL PARKS

(BY STATE)

ALABAMA

- Horseshoe Bend National Military Park (Daviston, AL)
- Little River Canyon National Preserve (Fort Payne, AL)
- Russell Cave National Monument (Bridgeport, AL)
- Selma to Montgomery National Historic Trail (Tuskegee, AL)
- Tuskegee Airmen National Historic Site (Tuskegee Institute, AL)
- Tuskegee Institute National Historic Site (Tuskegee Institute, AL)

ALASKA

- Alagnak Wild River (King Salmon, AK)
- Aleutian World War II National Historic Area (Unalaska, AK)
- Aniakchak National Monument & Preserve (King Salmon, AK)
- Bering Land Bridge National Preserve (Kotzebue, AK)
- Cape Krusenstern National Monument (Kotzebue, AK)
- Denali National Park & Preserve (Denali Park, AK)
- Gates of the Arctic National Park & Preserve (Bettles, AK)
- Glacier Bay National Park & Preserve (Gustavus, AK)
- Inupiat Heritage Center (Barrow, AK)
- Katmai National Park & Preserve (King Salmon, AK)
- Kenai Fjords National Park (Seward, AK)
- Klondike Gold Rush National Historical Park (Skagway, AK)
- Kobuk Valley National Park (Kotzebue, AK)
- Lake Clark National Park & Preserve (Port Alsworth, AK)
- Noatak National Preserve (Kotzebue, AK)
- Sitka National Historical Park (Sitka, AK)
- Western Arctic National Parklands (Kotzebue, AK)

- Wrangell–St. Elias National Park & Preserve (Copper Center, AK)
- Yukon–Charley Rivers National Preserve (Eagle, AK)

AMERICAN SAMOA

- National Park of American Samoa (Pago Pago, American Samoa, AS)

ARIZONA

- Canyon de Chelly National Monument (Chinle, AZ)
- Casa Grande Ruins National Monument (Coolidge, AZ)
- Chiricahua National Monument (Willcox, AZ)
- Coronado National Memorial (Hereford, AZ)
- Fort Bowie National Historic Site (Bowie, AZ)
- Glen Canyon National Recreation Area (Page, AZ)
- Grand Canyon National Park (Grand Canyon, AZ)
- Hohokam Pima National Monument (Coolidge, AZ)
- Hubbell Trading Post National Historic Site (Ganado, AZ)
- Montezuma Castle National Monument (Camp Verde, AZ)
- Navajo National Monument (Tonalea, AZ)
- Organ Pipe Cactus National Monument (Ajo, AZ)
- Petrified Forest National Park (Petrified Forest National Park, AZ)
- Pipe Spring National Monument (Fredonia, AZ)
- Saguaro National Park (Tucson, AZ)
- Sunset Crater Volcano National Monument (Flagstaff, AZ)
- Tonto National Monument (Roosevelt, AZ)
- Tumac cori National Historical Park (Tumacacori, AZ)
- Tuzigoot National Monument (Clarkdale, AZ)
- Walnut Canyon National Monument (Flagstaff, AZ)
- Wupatki National Monument (Flagstaff, AZ)

ARKANSAS

- Arkansas Post National Memorial (Gillett, AR)
- Buffalo National River (Harrison, AR)
- Central High School National Historic Site (Little Rock, AR)
- Fort Smith National Historic Site (Fort Smith, AR)
- Hot Springs National Park (Hot Springs, AR)
- Pea Ridge National Military Park (Pea Ridge, AR)

CALIFORNIA

- Alcatraz Island (San Francisco, CA)
- Cabrillo National Monument (San Diego, CA)
- Channel Islands National Park (Ventura, CA)
- Death Valley National Park (Death Valley, CA)
- Devils Postpile National Monument (Mammoth Lakes, CA)
- Eugene O'Neill National Historic Site (Danville, CA)
- Fort Point National Historic Site (Presidio of San Francisco, CA)
- Golden Gate National Recreation Area (San Francisco, CA)

- John Muir National Historic Site (Martinez, CA)
- Joshua Tree National Park (Twentynine Palms, CA)
- Juan Bautista De Anza National Historic Trail (Oakland, CA)
- Lassen Volcanic National Park (Mineral, CA)
- Lava Beds National Monument (Tulelake, CA)
- Manzanar National Historic Site (Independence, CA)
- Mojave National Preserve (Barstow, CA)
- Muir Woods National Monument (Mill Valley, CA)
- Pinnacles National Monument (Paicines, CA)
- Point Reyes National Seashore (Point Reyes, CA)
- Port Chicago Naval Magazine National Memorial (Danville, CA)
- Presidio of San Francisco (San Francisco, CA)
- Redwood National and State Parks (Crescent City, CA)
- Rosie the Riveter WWII Home Front National Historical Park (Oakland, CA)
- San Francisco Maritime National Historical Park (San Francisco, CA)
- Santa Monica Mountains National Recreation Area (Thousand Oaks, CA)
- Sequoia & Kings Canyon National Parks (Three Rivers, CA)
- Whiskeytown National Recreation Area (Whiskeytown, CA)
- Yosemite National Park (Sierra Nevada, CA)

COLORADO

- Bent's Old Fort National Historic Site (La Junta, CO)
- Black Canyon of the Gunnison National Park (Gunnison, CO)
- Colorado National Monument (Fruita, CO)
- Curecanti National Recreation Area (Gunnison, CO)
- Dinosaur National Monument (Dinosaur, CO)
- Florissant Fossil Beds National Monument (Florissant, CO)
- Great Sand Dunes National Monument & Preserve (Mosca, CO)
- Mesa Verde National Park (Mesa Verde National Park, CO)
- Rocky Mountain National Park (Estes Park, CO)
- Sand Creek Massacre National Historic Site (Eads, CO)
- Yucca House National Monument (Mesa Verde, CO)

CONNECTICUT

- Quinebaug & Shetucket Rivers Valley National Heritage Corridor (Putnam, CT)
- Weir Farm National Historic Site (Wilton, CT)

FLORIDA

- Big Cypress National Preserve (Ochopee, FL)
- Biscayne National Park (Homestead, FL)
- Canaveral National Seashore (Titusville, FL)
- Castillo de San Marcos National Monument (St. Augustine, FL)
- De Soto National Memorial (Bradenton, FL)
- Dry Tortugas National Park (Key West, FL)
- Everglades National Park (Homestead, FL)

- Fort Caroline National Memorial (Jacksonville, FL)
- Fort Matanzas National Monument (St. Augustine, FL)
- Gulf Islands National Seashore (Gulf Breeze, FL)
- Timucuan Ecological & Historic Preserve (Jacksonville, FL)

GEORGIA

- Andersonville National Historic Site (Andersonville, GA)
- Chattahoochee River National Recreation Area (Atlanta, GA)
- Chickamauga & Chattanooga National Military Park (Fort Oglethorpe, GA)
- Cumberland Island National Seashore (Saint Marys, GA)
- Fort Frederica National Monument (St. Simons Island, GA)
- Fort Pulaski National Monument (Savannah, GA)
- Jimmy Carter National Historic Site (Plains, GA)
- Kennesaw Mountain National Battlefield Park (Kennesaw, GA)
- Martin Luther King Jr. National Historic Site (Atlanta, GA)
- Ocmulgee National Monument (Macon, GA)
- Overmountain Victory National Historic Trail (Atlanta, GA)

GUAM

- War in the Pacific National Historical Park (Asan, GU)

HAWAII

- Haleakala National Park (Makawao, Maui, HI)
- Hawaii Volcanoes National Park (Hawaii National Park, HI)
- Kalaupapa National Historical Park (Kalaupapa, HI)
- Kaloko-Honokohau National Historical Park (Kailua-Kona, HI)
- Puukohola Heiau National Historic Site (Kawaihae, HI)
- Pu`uhonua O Honaunau National Historical Park (Honaunau, HI)
- USS *Arizona* Memorial (Honolulu, HI)

IDAHO

- City of Rocks National Reserve (Almo, ID)
- Craters of the Moon National Monument (Arco, ID)
- Hagerman Fossil Beds National Monument (Hagerman, ID)
- Nez Perce National Historical Park (Spalding, ID)

ILLINOIS

- Illinois & Michigan Canal National Heritage Corridor (Lockport, IL)
- Lincoln Home National Historic Site (Springfield, IL)

INDIANA

- George Rogers Clark National Historical Park (Vincennes, IN)
- Indiana Dunes National Lakeshore (Porter, IN)
- Lincoln Boyhood National Memorial (Lincoln City, IN)

IOWA

- Effigy Mounds National Monument (Harpers Ferry, IA)
- Herbert Hoover National Historic Site (West Branch, IA)

KANSAS

- Brown v Board of Education National Historic Site (Topeka, KS)

- Fort Larned National Historic Site (Larned, KS)
- Fort Scott National Historic Site (Fort Scott, KS)
- Nicodemus National Historic Site (Bogue, KS)
- Tallgrass Prairie National Preserve (Cottonwood Falls, KS)

KENTUCKY

- Abraham Lincoln Birthplace National Historic Site (Hodgenville, KY)
- Cumberland Gap National Historical Park (Middlesboro, KY)
- Mammoth Cave National Park (Mammoth Cave, KY)

LOUISIANA

- Cane River Creole National Historical Park (Natchitoches, LA)
- Cane River National Heritage Area (Natchitoches, LA)
- Jean Lafitte National Historic Park & Preserve (New Orleans, LA)
- New Orleans Jazz National Historical Park (New Orleans, LA)
- Poverty Point National Monument (Epps, LA)

MAINE

- Acadia National Park (Bar Harbor, ME)
- Maine Acadian Culture (Madawaska, ME)
- Roosevelt Campobello International Park (Lubec, ME)
- Saint Croix Island International Historic Site (Bar Harbor, ME)

MARIANAS

- American Memorial Park (Saipan, MP)

MARYLAND

- Antietam National Battlefield (Sharpsburg, MD)
- Antietam National Cemetery (Sharpsburg, MD)
- Assateague Island National Seashore (Berlin, MD)
- Baltimore-Washington Parkway (Greenbelt, MD)
- Catoctin Mountain Park (Thurmont, MD)
- Chesapeake & Ohio Canal National Historical Park (Hagerstown, MD)
- Clara Barton National Historic Site (Glen Echo, MD)
- Fort McHenry National Monument and Historic Shrine (Baltimore, MD)
- Fort Washington Park (Fort Washington, MD)
- Glen Echo Park (Glen Echo, MD)
- Greenbelt Park (Greenbelt, MD)
- Hampton National Historic Site (Towson, MD)
- Monocacy National Battlefield (Frederick, MD)
- Oxon Cove Park & Oxon Hill Farm (Oxon Hill, MD)
- Piscataway Park (Fort Washington, MD)
- Thomas Stone National Historic Site (Port Tobacco, MD)

MASSACHUSETTS

- Adams National Historical Park (Quincy, MA)
- Boston African American National Historic Site (Boston, MA)
- Boston Harbor Islands National Recreation Area (Boston, MA)
- Boston National Historical Park (Boston, MA)

- Cape Cod National Seashore (Wellfleet, MA)
- Frederick Law Olmsted National Historic Site (Brookline, MA)
- John F. Kennedy National Historic Site (Brookline, MA)
- Longfellow National Historic Site (Cambridge, MA)
- Lowell National Historical Park (Lowell, MA)
- Minute Man National Historical Park (Concord, MA)
- New Bedford Whaling National Historical Park (New Bedford, MA)
- Salem Maritime National Historic Site (Salem, MA)
- Saugus Iron Works National Historic Site (Saugus, MA)
- Springfield Armory National Historic Site (Springfield, MA)

MICHIGAN

- Father Marquette National Memorial (St. Ignace, MI)
- Isle Royale National Park (Houghton, MI)
- Keweenaw National Historical Park (Calumet, MI)
- Pictured Rocks National Lakeshore (Munising, MI)
- Sleeping Bear Dunes National Lakeshore (Empire, MI)

MINNESOTA

- Grand Portage National Monument (Grand Marais, MN)
- Mississippi National River & Recreation Area (St. Paul, MN)
- Pipestone National Monument (Pipestone, MN)
- Voyageurs National Park (International Falls, MN)

MISSISSIPPI

- Brices Cross Roads National Battlefield Site (Tupelo, MS)
- Natchez National Historical Park (Natchez, MS)
- Natchez Trace Parkway (Tupelo, MS)
- Tupelo National Battlefield (Tupelo, MS)
- Vicksburg National Cemetery (Vicksburg, MS)
- Vicksburg National Military Park (Vicksburg, MS)

MISSOURI

- George Washington Carver National Monument (Diamond, MO)
- Harry S. Truman National Historic Site (Independence, MO)
- Jefferson National Expansion Memorial (St. Louis, MO)
- Ozark National Scenic Riverways (Van Buren, MO)
- Ulysses S. Grant National Historic Site (St. Louis, MO)
- Wilson's Creek National Battlefield (Republic, MO)

MONTANA

- Big Hole National Battlefield (Wisdom, MT)
- Bighorn Canyon National Recreation Area (Fort Smith, MT)
- Glacier National Park (West Glacier, MT)
- Grant-Kohrs Ranch National Historic Site (Deer Lodge, MT)
- Little Bighorn Battlefield National Monument (Crow Agency, MT)

NEBRASKA

- Agate Fossil Beds National Monument (Harrison, NE)

- Chimney Rock National Historic Site (Bayard, NE)
- Homestead National Monument of America (Beatrice, NE)
- Lewis & Clark National Historic Trail (Omaha, NE)
- Missouri National Recreational River (O'Neill, NE)
- Niobrara National Scenic River, (O'Neill, NE)
- Scotts Bluff National Monument (Gering, NE)

NEVADA

- Great Basin National Park (Baker, NV)
- Lake Mead National Recreation Area (Boulder City, NV)
- Parashant National Monument (Boulder City, NV)

NEW HAMPSHIRE

- Saint-Gaudens National Historic Site (Cornish, NH)

NEW JERSEY

- Edison National Historic Site (West Orange, NJ)
- Morristown National Historical Park (Morristown, NJ)
- New Jersey Coastal Heritage Trail Route (Newport, NJ)

NEW MEXICO

- Aztec Ruins National Monument (Aztec, NM)
- Bandelier National Monument (Los Alamos, NM)
- Capulin Volcano National Monument (Capulin, NM)
- Carlsbad Caverns National Park (Carlsbad, NM)
- Chaco Culture National Historical Park (Nageezi, NM)
- El Camino Real de Tierra Adentro National Historic Trail (Santa Fe, NM)
- El Malpais National Monument (Grants, NM)
- El Morro National Monument (Ramah, NM)
- Fort Union National Monument (Watrous, NM)
- Gila Cliff Dwellings National Monument (Silver City, NM)
- Pecos National Historical Park (Pecos, NM)
- Petroglyph National Monument (Albuquerque, NM)
- Salinas Pueblo Missions National Monument (Mountainair, NM)
- Santa Fe National Historic Trail (Santa Fe, NM)
- Trail of Tears National Historic Trail (Santa Fe, NM)
- White Sands National Monument (Holloman AFB, NM)

NEW YORK

- Castle Clinton National Monument (New York, NY)
- Eleanor Roosevelt National Historic Site (Hyde Park, NY)
- Ellis Island National Monument (New York, NY)
- Erie Canalway National Heritage Corridor (Waterford, NY)
- Federal Hall National Memorial (New York, NY)
- Fire Island National Seashore (Patchogue, NY)
- Fort Stanwix National Monument (Rome, NY)

- Gateway National Recreation Area (Staten Island, NY)
- General Grant National Memorial (New York, NY)
- Hamilton Grange National Memorial (New York, NY)
- Home Of Franklin Delano Roosevelt National Historic Site (Hyde Park, NY)
- Lower East Side Tenement Museum National Historic Site (New York, NY)
- Manhattan Sites (New York, NY)
- Martin Van Buren National Historic Site (Kinderhook, NY)
- Sagamore Hill National Historic Site (Oyster Bay, NY)
- Saint Paul's Church National Historic Site (Mount Vernon, NY)
- Saratoga National Historical Park (Stillwater, NY)
- Statue of Liberty National Monument (New York, NY)
- Theodore Roosevelt Birthplace National Historic Site (New York, NY)
- Theodore Roosevelt Inaugural National Historic Site (Buffalo, NY)
- Vanderbilt Mansion National Historic Site (Hyde Park, NY)
- Women's Rights National Historical Park (Seneca Falls, NY)

NORTH CAROLINA

- Blue Ridge Parkway (Asheville, NC)
- Cape Hatteras National Seashore (Manteo, NC)
- Cape Lookout National Seashore (Harkers Island, NC)
- Carl Sandburg Home National Historic Site (Flat Rock, NC)
- Fort Raleigh National Historic Site (Manteo, NC)
- Guilford Courthouse National Military Park (Greensboro, NC)
- Moores Creek National Battlefield (Currie, NC)
- Wright Brothers National Memorial (Manteo, NC)

NORTH DAKOTA

- Fort Union Trading Post National Historic Site (Williston, ND)
- Knife River Indian Villages National Historic Site (Stanton, ND)
- Theodore Roosevelt National Park (Medora, ND)

OHIO

- Cuyahoga Valley National Park (Brecksville, OH)
- David Berger National Memorial (Cleveland Heights, OH)
- Dayton Aviation Heritage National Historical Park (Dayton, OH)
- First Ladies National Historic Site (Canton, OH)
- Hopewell Culture National Historical Park (Chillicothe, OH)
- James A. Garfield National Historic Site (Mentor, OH)
- Perry's Victory & International Peace Memorial (Put-in-Bay, OH)
- William Howard Taft National Historic Site (Cincinnati, OH)

OKLAHOMA

- Chickasaw National Recreation Area (Sulphur, OK)
- Oklahoma City National Memorial (Oklahoma City, OK)
- Washita Battlefield National Historic Site (Cheyenne, OK)

OREGON

- Crater Lake National Park (Crater Lake, OR)
- Fort Clatsop National Memorial (Astoria, OR)
- John Day Fossil Beds National Monument (Kimberly, OR)
- Oregon Caves National Monument (Cave Junction, OR)

PENNSYLVANIA

- Allegheny Portage Railroad National Historic Site (Gallitzin, PA)
- Delaware & Lehigh National Heritage Corridor (Easton, PA)
- Delaware National Scenic River (Bushkill, PA)
- Delaware Water Gap National Recreation Area (Bushkill, PA)
- Deshler-Morris House (Philadelphia, PA)
- Edgar Allan Poe National Historic Site (Philadelphia, PA)
- Eisenhower National Historic Site (Gettysburg, PA)
- Fort Necessity National Battlefield (Farmington, PA)
- Friendship Hill National Historic Site (Point Marion, PA)
- Gettysburg National Cemetery (Gettysburg, PA)
- Gettysburg National Military Park (Gettysburg, PA)
- Gloria Dei Church National Historic Site (Philadelphia, PA)
- Hopewell Furnace National Historic Site (Elverson, PA)
- Independence National Historical Park (Philadelphia, PA)
- Johnstown Flood National Memorial (South Fork, PA)
- New Jersey Pinelands National Reserve (Philadelphia, PA)
- Steamtown National Historic Site (Scranton, PA)
- Thaddeus Kosciuszko National Memorial (Philadelphia, PA)
- Upper Delaware Scenic & Recreational River (Beach Lake, PA)
- Valley Forge National Historical Park (Valley Forge, PA)

PUERTO RICO

- San Juan National Historic Site (San Juan, PR)

RHODE ISLAND

- Blackstone River Valley National Heritage Corridor (Woonsocket, RI)
- Roger Williams National Memorial (Providence, RI)
- Touro Synagogue National Historic Site (Newport, RI)

SOUTH CAROLINA

- Charles Pinckney National Historic Site (Sullivans Island, SC)
- Congaree Swamp National Monument (Hopkins, SC)
- Cowpens National Battlefield (Chesnee, SC)
- Fort Moultrie National Monument (Sullivan's Island, SC)
- Fort Sumter National Monument (Sullivan's Island, SC)
- Kings Mountain National Military Park (Blacksburg, SC)
- Ninety Six National Historic Site (Ninety Six, SC)

SOUTH DAKOTA

- Badlands National Park (Interior, SD)
- Jewel Cave National Monument (Custer, SD)
- Minuteman Missile National Historic Site (Interior, SD)
- Mount Rushmore National Memorial (Keystone, SD)
- Wind Cave National Park (Hot Springs, SD)

TENNESSEE

- Andrew Johnson National Historic Site (Greeneville, TN)
- Big South Fork National River & Recreation Area (Oneida, TN)
- Fort Donelson National Battlefield (Dover, TN)
- Fort Donelson National Cemetery (Dover, TN)
- Great Smoky Mountains National Park (Gatlinburg, TN)
- Obed Wild & Scenic River (Wartburg, TN)
- Shiloh National Cemetery (Shiloh, TN)
- Shiloh National Military Park (Shiloh, TN)
- Stones River National Battlefield (Murfreesboro, TN)
- Stones River National Cemetery (Murfreesboro, TN)

TEXAS

- Alibates Flint Quarries National Monument (Fritch, TX)
- Amistad National Recreation Area (Del Rio, TX)
- Big Bend National Park (Big Bend National Park, TX)
- Big Thicket National Preserve (Beaumont, TX)
- Chamizal National Memorial (El Paso, TX)
- Fort Davis National Historic Site (Fort Davis, TX)
- Guadalupe Mountains National Park (Salt Flat, TX)
- Lake Meredith National Recreation Area (Fritch, TX)
- Lyndon B. Johnson National Historical Park (Johnson City, TX)
- Padre Island National Seashore (Corpus Christi, TX)
- Palo Alto Battlefield National Historic Site (Brownsville, TX)
- Rio Grande Wild & Scenic River (Big Bend National Park, TX)
- San Antonio Missions National Historical Park (San Antonio, TX)

UTAH

- Arches National Park (Moab, UT)
- Bryce Canyon National Park (Bryce Canyon, UT)
- California National Historic Trail (Salt Lake City, UT)
- Canyonlands National Park (Moab, UT)
- Capitol Reef National Park (Torrey, UT)
- Cedar Breaks National Monument (Cedar City, UT)
- Golden Spike National Historic Site (Brigham City, UT)
- Mormon Pioneer National Historic Trail (Salt Lake City, UT)
- Natural Bridges National Monument (Lake Powell, UT)
- Pony Express National Historic Trail (Salt Lake City, UT)
- Timpanogos Cave National Monument (American Fork, UT)
- Zion National Park (Springdale, UT)

VERMONT

- Marsh-Billings-Rockefeller National Historical Park (Woodstock, VT)

VIRGIN ISLANDS

- Buck Island Reef National Monument (Christiansted, St. Croix, VI)
- Christiansted National Historic Site (Christiansted, St. Croix, VI)
- Salt River Bay National Historic Park and Ecological Preserve (Christiansted, VI)
- Virgin Islands National Park (St. John, VI)

VIRGINIA

- Appomattox Court House National Historical Park (Appomattox, VA)
- Arlington House, The Robert E. Lee Memorial (McLean, VA)
- Booker T. Washington National Monument (Hardy, VA)
- Cape Henry National Memorial (Yorktown, VA)
- Claude Moore Colonial Farm (McLean, VA)
- Colonial National Historical Park (Yorktown, VA)
- Fredericksburg & Spotsylvania National Military Park (Fredericksburg, VA)
- Fredericksburg National Cemetery (Fredericksburg, VA)
- George Washington Birthplace National Monument (Washington's Birthplace, VA)
- George Washington Memorial Parkway (McLean, VA)
- Great Falls Park (McLean, VA)
- Green Springs (Elkton, VA)
- Jamestown National Historic Site (Yorktown, VA)
- Lyndon Baines Johnson Memorial Grove on the Potomac (McLean, VA)
- Maggie L. Walker National Historic Site (Richmond, VA)
- Manassas National Battlefield Park (Manassas, VA)
- Petersburg National Battlefield (Petersburg, VA)
- Poplar Grove National Cemetery (Petersburg, VA)
- Prince William Forest Park (Triangle, VA)
- Richmond National Battlefield Park (Richmond, VA)
- Shenandoah National Park (Luray, VA)
- Theodore Roosevelt Island Park (McLean, VA)
- Wolf Trap Farm Park for the Performing Arts (Vienna, VA)
- Yorktown National Battlefield (Yorktown, VA)
- Yorktown National Cemetery (Yorktown, VA)

WASHINGTON

- Ebey's Landing National Historical Reserve (Coupeville, WA)
- Fort Vancouver National Historic Site (Vancouver, WA)
- Franklin D. Roosevelt Lake (Coulee Dam, WA)
- Klondike Gold Rush–Seattle Unit National Historical Park (Seattle, WA)
- Lake Chelan National Recreation Area (Sedro-Woolley, WA)
- Mount Rainier National Park (Ashford, WA)
- North Cascades National Park (Sedro-Woolley, WA)
- Olympic National Park (Port Angeles, WA)
- Ross Lake National Recreation Area (Sedro-Woolley, WA)

- San Juan Island National Historical Park (Friday Harbor, WA)
- Whitman Mission National Historic Site (Walla Walla, WA)

WASHINGTON, DC

- Anacostia Park (Washington, DC)
- Battleground National Cemetery (Washington, DC)
- Constitution Gardens (Washington, DC)
- Ford's Theatre National Historic Site (Washington, DC)
- Fort Dupont Park (Washington, DC)
- Franklin Delano Roosevelt Memorial (Washington, DC)
- Frederick Douglass National Historic Site (Washington, DC)
- Kenilworth Park & Aquatic Gardens (Washington, DC)
- Korean War Veterans Memorial (Washington, DC)
- Lincoln Memorial (Washington, DC)
- Mary McLeod Bethune Council House National Historic Site (Washington, DC)
- National Capital Parks-Central (Washington, DC)
- National Capital Parks-East (Washington, DC)
- National Mall (Washington, DC)
- Old Post Office Tower (Washington, DC)
- The Old Stone House (Washington, DC)
- Peirce Mill (Washington, DC)
- Pennsylvania Avenue National Historic Site (Washington, DC)
- President's Park (White House) (Washington, DC)
- Rock Creek Park (Washington, DC)
- Sewall-Belmont House National Historic Site (Washington, DC)
- Thomas Jefferson Memorial (Washington, DC)
- Vietnam Veterans Memorial (Washington, DC)
- Washington Monument (Washington, DC)

WEST VIRGINIA

- Appalachian National Scenic Trail (Harpers Ferry, WV)
- Bluestone National Scenic River (Glen Jean, WV)
- Gauley River National Recreation Area (Glen Jean, WV)
- Harpers Ferry National Historical Park (Harpers Ferry, WV)
- New River Gorge National River (Glen Jean, WV)
- Potomac Heritage National Scenic Trail (Harpers Ferry, WV)

WISCONSIN

- Apostle Islands National Lakeshore (Bayfield, WI)
- Ice Age National Scenic Trail (Madison, WI)
- North Country National Scenic Trail (Madison, WI)
- Saint Croix National Scenic River (Saint Croix Falls, WI)

WYOMING

- Devils Tower National Monument (Devils Tower, WY)
- Fort Laramie National Historic Site (Fort Laramie, WY)
- Fossil Butte National Monument (Kemmerer, WY)
- Grand Teton National Park (Moose, WY)
- John D. Rockefeller Jr. Memorial Parkway (Moose, WY)
- Yellowstone National Park (Yellowstone National Park, WY)

design by jan derevjanik

illustrations by laura palese

written by jennifer defillipi and jean lynch

www.clarksonpotter.com

isbn: 1-4000-5212-2

potter style